Published by Crooked Wall Press
Copyright © 2022 Leslie J. Anderson
All rights reserved
ISBN: 9798367624915

Cover Illustration: Helvetica Blanc "Diadem" 2022

# Take This to Space

Leslie J. Anderson

Dedicated to Jarod and Arthur,
the very best things on this planet.

# Forword
## by Jarod K. Anderson

It feels reductive to say that Leslie is a poet of awe.

She is.

But the connotations of that word have become cold, three letters lying dead on a page.

Leslie unpacks awe and in the unpacking we find more than just wonder and amazement, more than just glossy images of distant galaxies and comic book legends.

She coaxes us to look closer, to zoom-in on the postcard perfection until we see pores, until we see sweat, tears, and constellations of fresh wounds and puckered scars.

In this collection, we are reminded what else we may find when we don't allow ourselves to stop at simple wonder.

We find grief, the keen sadness of having our fingertips graze what we could become and then falling short.

We find anger at all the miraculous joys locked behind gatekeepers and relegated to claustrophobic little contexts, wonders held captive by little boys of all sizes.

We find a deep love and longing for fully-impossible things that teeter on the knife's edge of transformation into nearly-impossible things, into once-thought-impossible things.

We find fear.

"Awe" metastasizing into "awful," into terrible kinds of understanding.

There is awe in the cultural alchemy that turns women into things, into robots and set dressing.

There is awe in understanding how abuse can poison new love or turn our half-remembered homeworlds into glittering explosions suspended in a field of stars.

Leslie's awe often arrives packaged in her childhood passions: horses and Star Wars and superheroes and silver spaceships speeding toward alien worlds.

Yet, these things aren't set before us as cheap paths to world-weary cynicism or tiresome ironic detachment.

I called them childhood passions, but Leslie rarely seems eager to make such distinctions.

Leslie loves and honors these things, woman and child, and is not interested in apologizing for it. Instead, she says, "no, these are my cherished allies and legends and my growth is their growth, my journey is their journey too."

These poems make it clear that lightsabers and Supergirl, that ponies and rocketships were there for Leslie when she needed them (and they still are).

It is deeply refreshing that she refuses to shy away from the respect these relationships merit, that she is strong enough to say that the meaning we make, the meaning that keeps us whole, deserves our continued respect and engagement.

In this sense, I find these poems to be both natural and aspirational.

It is, perhaps, strange that I think of Leslie as a nature poet, but I do.

Superficially, it doesn't make any sense.

It makes sense to me.

It makes sense because nature is not just wildflower meadows and forested hillsides.

Nature is distant galaxies that share a family resemblance with our own.

Nature is the very human drive to see what is beyond the next valley or the next solar system.

Nature is our ability to build the meaning we need for the life we face, to build it the way beavers craft their own rich wetlands.

Nature is falling in love.

Nature is scar tissue.

Nature is mourning what we are not even as we feel pulled toward the intoxicating quest to discover what we may become.

Leslie is a nature poet.

She is a poet of awe and of fierce grief.

She is something else entirely, something from the pages of a comic, something like an ink-splash in the dark between the stars, something that calls us to gallop toward the horizon, to beguile physics and build the rockets, to follow our childhood heroes and go see what is out there, to see what the artist made magic by leaving it mostly undrawn.

# Table of Contents

Forward ·············································································· 6
Manifesto ·········································································· 12
Truth as Simple as Rockets ············································· 13
The Amazing Mystery Women ········································ 14
Oh, Smallest Future ························································ 15
Little Red Wolf ································································ 16
Magical Girl Transformation ·········································· 17
I Took a Quiz on the Internet ········································ 18
Abduction ········································································ 19
Let Me Explain the Sin ·················································· 20
The Heavenly Body ························································ 21
What I Have Done for my Husband Today ·················· 22
Advice to a New Parent ················································ 23
Princess Leia, Mother of My Anger······························· 24
Medusa Told Me ···························································· 26
Supergirl Doesn't Look at the Stars······························· 27
Climate ············································································ 28
I Know You Want to Lie by The Roadside but the Wolves ··· 29
Grind ··············································································· 30
What a Tree ··································································· 31
Sirens Don't Drown Men················································ 32
In the Valley of Midas···················································· 33
Post Apocalyptic ···························································· 34
Your Homeworld is Gone··············································· 35
The Most Original Sin ···················································· 36
Grace ············································································· 37
Sleeping Beauty Attains Bliss ········································ 38
Refugee··········································································· 40
Supergirl Mourns Krypton ·············································· 41
Interior Design································································· 42
For Want of Prophecy in Delphi ··································· 43
The Exquisite Banality of Space ··································· 44
The Rocket Falls to ······················································· 45
Ponies and Rocketships ················································ 46
Launch ············································································ 49
Weight ············································································ 50
Float ················································································ 51
I Will Try to Describe····················································· 52
Microbiome ····································································· 53

| | |
|---|---|
| No Place for Us But the Place We Stand Upon | 54 |
| Ars Fucking Poetica | 55 |
| Wonder Woman Visits the City | 56 |
| Rey the Sister of My Strength | 57 |
| Loss Like Empty Seeds | 58 |
| A Spell | 60 |
| They Threw Tomato Soup on the Sunflowers | 61 |
| Tell Me What the Stars Sing | 62 |
| Cassini | 63 |
| Ballón de la Luna | 64 |
| Supergirl's Last Will and Testament | 65 |
| Divine | 66 |
| The Plagues | 68 |
| Werewolf's Aubade | 70 |
| Center | 71 |
| The Encyclopedia of Completely Normal Planets | 72 |
| The Pig, Wilbur, to His Grandsons | 73 |
| Potato Song | 74 |
| Eulogy for Spirit and Opportunity | 75 |
| They Didn't Hate You Because You Read Comics | 76 |
| Big Bang | 78 |
| Deerborn | 79 |
| Not Helen but the Thing that Held Her | 80 |
| Siren Song | 82 |
| The Ghost of an Astronaut Talking to the Ghost of a Cowgirl | 83 |
| As Salmon Swim Upstream | 84 |
| Acknowledgements | 86 |
| About the Author | 89 |

# Manifesto

Out behind the white house,
so small, wrapped in a blanket,
I saw the stars dripping down
the mouth of the universe
like honey.

Up there,
the ISS spins like a dandelion seed.
It's been more than a decade
since we were all home –
all humans on the same planet.
Maybe it will never happen again.

Feel now the fire, the great fire,
pushing us into the sky
like a needle.

It is our inheritance,
our obligation
to leave our home behind.

There is nothing greater
than this –
the thing that we already are.

# Truth as Simple as Rockets

My uncle asks me if I resent
that I write about space but will never go.
Does it bother me that I chose
the wrong profession?
He is drunk and therefor mean
and my aunt says
*Matthew* in the tone of *stop* and I say
No no it's fine. I wouldn't pass
testing anyway – my eyes for one –
and isn't it wonderful
to receive the gift of everything
from a complete stranger?

To read and see and collect the carefully
managed notes of the universe
from another's hand? From a teammate? It is generosity
in the infinite. It is humanity
in perfection.

But also
Also.
*I do.*

# The Amazing Mystery Women

They have pink hair in one panel,
blonde the next. They wear
nothing or silk babydoll dresses.
Their hips are to the side.

They do not sit. They drape,
they lounge, they sip. They love
each other like parakeets in
a cage. Bruce Wayne holds one in his hand
like a tissue.

One of them dated the Riddler once.
She remembers him as a little distracted.
They never quite hit it off. He doesn't
think of her.

*How is a woman like a bullet, Batman?*

The Amazing Mystery Women
stand in the background –
cry because someone is shooting at them.

The Amazing Mystery Women vomit and bleed,
but you don't see that.
Only the naked skin, the broken coffee table, the inevitable
screaming.

*A woman is like a bullet, Batman.*

*Don't worry about the ones
that aren't for you.*

# Oh, Smallest Future

You are a crystal ball
in the nest of my intestines.

At night I move my hands
over the arch of my horizon –
blindly, reading the future
through a red curtain.

I'm learning you
through the veil
of my own body.

You are symptoms –
vomit, pain, a swelling
of everything, pink
and purple veined.

I try to tell your future,
to read the phrenology
of my stomach, the ornithomancy
of my bulging veins.

I hope it is a gentle future,
little one. But for now
you are a secret
I am keeping
from myself.

# Little Red Wolf

Her mother said
fold your ears,
keep your nose
in your hood,
look down
when you walk,
tuck your hands
under the basket.

She did all these things.
She forgot her voice.
Her fur itched.
The wool
was thick and hot.

When she opened the door,
there were the eyes, the teeth,
the smell of wet fur and earth.

She said
*I know you,*
and the joy was as great
as the fear.

# Magical Girl Transformation

Light will divide you
into what you were
and what you will be
and that cut
will be different every time.

The fractals slip between
your atoms
like barn swallows.

As you shimmer
through the darkness
you glance behind you.
Maybe you dropped
yourself.

And one day you might
see your reflection
in skyscrapers, or a still pond,
a blade in your hands
and silver in your eyes
and think,
*what would I think
of what I have become?*

And you won't remember.
You won't recall
what it felt like
to be that kind of you.

# I Took a Quiz on the Internet

and it asked
where are you right now?
Where would you like to be?
Here is a forest.
Here is a cabin.
You are a tree with a blanket underneath.
Place these on your heart and see
if a light turns on.

Isn't wonderful that we can do
this silly thing while we eat
a silly lunch?

Isn't it nice that there are things
which just exist? That we
can hold up to the sun
and see what colors they make?

This is why I write, you know.
This is why I do
anything.

What color are you?
A white mug.
Salt and bread.
Gratitude.

# Abduction

Cows have seen more space than us.
For generations they were lifted
into the delicate, spinning stars,
their soft heads raised, loamy eyes
watching calmly, not quite curious.

The ships, like ornaments, rocked
on their inconspicuous, black hooks.
The cows' hooves left the ground.
They were held by light as they remembered
being held as calves.
Maybe they kicked once, testing for something solid,
found nothing, were still.

In the glistening laboratory
they ruminated on the last bit of earth
in their stomachs,
watched out the window.
The vastness of space
shrieked past like jack rabbits.

As the silver knives grew closer,
they probably considered infinity;
they thought they might have seen it once before
in the black of their mother's eye,
or the cold, damp dirt under the winter ice.
And though all of humanity wonders
at the pain or joy or glory or retribution
of being carried into the sky, the cows
have not thought any of these things. They thought, maybe,
*this is not a terrible place to go.*

# Let Me Explain the Sin

The first one,
the big one,
was the moment Eve became
inhuman –

shattering,
kaleidoscope-like,
into an infinity of not-man.

The knowledge we swallowed was
the ability
to lick the offense
like a stamp
and stick it
to one of those diagonals of being
that we swore was unlike
ourselves –

the beginning of
other –

Adam looking at his twin,
his partner, his mirror
and saying,
(the apple's juice
dripping down his neck
rotting in his stomach),

What have
you
done?

# The Heavenly Body

When food becomes numbers,
when warm rice
and salt and lemon juice
are quantified,
they become ghosts
on the tongue.
In the sky, hungry,
the moon dreams of sewing
the furniture to the wall.
She wanes. She becomes
sharp. Hunger does not bring
clarity. The bed pulses
brackish and oily.
The night consumes
her. Everything is reduced
to its measurable amount.
In the end we are
equations in a single
equation. A zero.
A whole and a
void.

# What I Have Done for my Husband Today

I started coffee,
decided which mug to put it in –
acorn or starfish.
I wrote *good morning* on the yellow pad,
even though it wasn't morning,
but last night was hard and this day
is now new.
Definitely acorns, usually acorns,
like we used gather and put in our pockets
for nothing, for fun, to line up along the top of the stove.
I moved his keys from under his hat
so he wouldn't miss them.
In this house we do not take for granted
what might be missed.
In this house we do not take for granted
that we are leaving someone
alone in one of the rooms.
I wave at the security camera before we leave
so when he checks the video he will see me
fluttering at an empty room,
mouthing *I love you* to no one,
for nothing,
again,
just in case.

# Advice to a New Parent

Having a child destroys you,
but everything destroys you.
The air will unravel you
given enough time
and exposure.
Change is inevitable.
You are already
a million deaths.
You have simply
created a new agent of your
metamorphosis
and it is
growing.

# Princess Leia, Mother of My Anger

Leia, Leia! You were my
rebellion.
I punched a classmate
in the mouth for you, Leia –
wearing knee socks and buckle shoes.

He called you weak.
He said if I wanted to be you
so badly
I could wait by the chestnut tree
to be rescued.
I hit him to the ground, Leia.
He told the lunch lady.
I sat in the hall
and I was not ashamed.

I wanted to be you
so badly.

I watched New Hope
in a theater where my feet
didn't touch the floor.
Your ship
roared over my head.
Leia, you lied to a man
who wanted to hurt you.
I knew what that felt like.

You were the first
banner before me.
Leia,
I never asked
if I could follow.
I just followed.

Your anger looked
like my anger.
I chewed it and swallowed it.
I felt it flow through me.

And while everyone fell
to their fury, not you.
Not me.
It galvanized and gilded
you. Leia,
I am crying in the library.
Leia,

crying again, Leia, like I did
with my lightsaber lunch box
and a bruise over my eye,
like you did for your homeworld
quietly, off-screen.

# Medusa Told Me

There is a trick
to turning men to stone,
she said. Come here.
let me braid
your hair.
I'll tell you.

When they look at you
but see only
your skin or hair
or legs or breasts
and tell you so
you must feel
all the anger
you feel.

Let the ritual burn.
Let the smoke fill
the temple
of you.

Scream at them
or not. It doesn't
matter.
The magic is done.

I told her, *Medusa*
*I already do this.*
*Nothing happens.*

She kissed me,
The tongues of her snakes
whispered against my skin.

Oh, sweetheart,
somewhere
those men are turning
gray and hard.
They are dying
of you.

# Supergirl Doesn't Look at the Stars

The light
from her planet's death
is still there,
still traveling
toward her,
300,000 kilometers
per second.

She cannot
outrun it.

The stars above her
pulse, burn, crash.
So many are ghosts.

She saves a hundred,
thousand,
million
people.
None of them
know her name.

None of them know
grief
is the gravity
of the finite.

The universe
forgets in long form.

# Climate

It was always going to be
the sea that came for us.

Driving home, I
feel the air rise up
on its haunches.

What I thought was a flock of birds
is a cloud of smoke.

I stare at the bloodshot roadkill
like running my tongue
over and over a cavity.

The radio says
our flood risk is medium
and rising,

but the sea was always here
in our red insides.
It has seen
everything we've done.

# I Know You Want to Lie by The Roadside but the Wolves Are Coming, Sweetheart

I'm here with you.
Our feet are bare at the beginning of a long walk.

I know the field looks empty now.
It's not. The seeds are still growing.

Do not learn the lessons of heartbreak.
The wisdom of sorrow is a lie.

It will tell you wolves are a mercy,
that a bare field is acceptable.

If you need to rest let's do it now.
Drink water, sleep, hold yourself.
Save your voice for when it's time to scream.

I won't lie to you, though.
The wolves are coming.

In your heart is a knife
but also a harvest.

When it's time,
use one to protect
the other.

# Grind

Rumi wrote
*What you are*
*seeking is also seeking you.*

You skipped lunch again.
Sleep is a sip of warm water.

Your dreams have teeth.
They are the starving children
of your parent's hunger.

Blessed are those
who are never
satisfied, taking mouthfuls
of ourselves –
chewing.

It's dark when you arrive,
dark when you go.
You race to your car
with your keys between your fingers.

You know what's
out there.

While you're
following your dreams,
they are following you.

They are hungry.
You are outnumbered.

# What a Tree

At the edge of the parking lot
stands an oak taller than the office building.
I pity it, I think.
What a stony place to grow – over a lake
of black and gray and yellow.

But how dare I?
It is tall and proud.
It is in control of its life.
It could decide next spring
not to produce a single leaf,
live out the summer,
and then die from dehydration.

Instead, it has gone and produced little trees –
thrown them in the wind like a child throws tissue.
It goes on, like I do, nature in nature
regardless of our proximity.

It is tempting to say
*Those creeping roots have cracked the pavement.*
*They have snuck into the foundation.*
But probably the tree just goes on living
beside its strange neighbors.
It probably doesn't think of me at all.

# Sirens Don't Drown Men

It is the sea.

It was not the sun that killed Icarus,
but the waves.

Your love does not destroy you;
the void in its wake will pull you under.

You will remember the leaving,
a bowl in the sink,
a shadow that does not fall.

The world tends toward endings.
The sea is still the sea.

# In the Valley of Midas

You cannot build anything soft
that does not become hard.
Even the stories turn into gold,
running down the peoples' throats.
They cough red and yellow
into handkerchiefs,
drop them into the sewers.
The very dust –
microscopic cubes of gold,
stick in their lungs.
Food must be eaten quickly.
As it touches the tongue
it begins to taste like words, like truth,
like blood, like everything
in this place.
Some children are born statues.
Some look at the world
blindly, with gilded eyes.
Around this valley lies a golden wall.
They believe it is to keep people out.

# Post Apocalyptic

The universe is soaked in time,
dripping with it.
It clogs the galaxies and nebulas.

And, blurbling out from it,
life turns and stares
in awe.

Every year we traveled around the sun.
We voyage.
We explore.
We see the neighboring stars
and our sister, the moon.

We have survived the end of worlds.
They have blinked out far away
and we have lived on,
and will,
and won't.

# Your Homeworld is Gone

The sand from your childhood
is in the ocean now,
in glass, on the rugs
of a man in Seattle,
a woman in Mumbai.

The carbon you wear
is borrowed.
Your molecules,
the pathways of your mind,
shift like dunes.

This sky is not
the one you remember,
and even memory
drifts.

There is no home,
not the home you knew.

There is no you,
not the one you remember.

The ground itself
will give way.
Congratulations,
you are like everything.

# The Most Original Sin

If heaven is real,
if Eve is real,
I hope she doesn't feel
guilty.

I hope she is angry
that her children suffer
for apples.

I hope she gives God that look
over her nose that makes him
squirm.

*Don't look at me like that,* God says.

*Mmhm.* Eve answers.

I hope she holds us
in heaven, when we get there,
bleeding and screaming.
I hope she tells us
she loves us no matter what.

She grasps our hands as we
are judged, looks at Peter
like he knows what he did
and how dare he?

I hope she never steps on the serpent –
never ever.
I hope she coaxes him into a cup,
slides a newspaper underneath,
and dumps him outside.

# Grace

It is not rising above.
It is not the moon.
It is not a white breath,
a wing,
a crowned heart,
a golden snake.

It is,
with your own blood
running down your legs,
the dirt caked
on your hands,
walking,
walking,
walking.

# Sleeping Beauty Attains Bliss

Once I fussed at my hair, my nails,
the little silver tassels of my cloak –
everything bright and straight –

Then I pricked my finger on the spindle
of a spinning wheel. No one came
for me.
The end.

I lay on my back as the ants crawled over my skin,
their fragile nothingness
as perfect as me –
as complete.
I stared at the canopy of midnight blue
as it faded to gray, and wondered.

Then, running out of things to wonder, I let white
settle over my mind like a wedding veil.

Let me say, that ephemeral beauty was
so essential. Now though, there are other things
first in my mind –
I am a ruby set in the golden crown
of time.

The thorns that choked the garden path
crawled into the window.
The little red flowers
bloomed in an instant and died.

Nothing lasts –
Not white horses, nor carriages,
crowns nor swords, not kisses
on my lips. I smile for no one
but my beautiful, eternal self.

Now, everyone has forgotten me.
I'll probably be here until everything

becomes light and sound and lifts away.

Don't be afraid
to be glad for me. We must accept
wherever we find peace in this life,
even alone, trying to open our eyes.

# Refugee

Before Wonder Woman
dragged the first man
onto the shores
of Themyscira,

the inhabitants liked
to watch the men
drown.

When the planes
or boats
or tiny rafts
crashed into the black rocks
that ringed their shores
like a dark crown,

the Amazons
gathered to sing,
to write poems,
to mourn
as a group.
The men
in the water
cried
for their mothers.

*What was a mother?*
they wondered,
and,
*Isn't it sad,*
*so sad,*
*so poetically sad?*
*It is so lovely*
*here in our paradise*
*to feel a sadness*
*almost real.*

# Supergirl Mourns Krypton

The fox on the other side
of the fence gives the dogs
nightmares.

They toss and turn in my bed.

In the morning I think
I will kill it, but
it is lying in the yellow sun
red as a laser.

These humans
build houses out of space –
build walls around nothing –
call this inside.

*Kara, come inside.*

There's a place you can't reach
unless you carry a weight
you can't bear.

It is a field in Kansas.

The fox wanders off. The dogs
won't leave me.
The humans bring me dinner.

They want to know
if I need anything.

Nothing and yes.

# Interior Design

In the summer of 2001, the barn flooded
and by the time we got to the grain
the bottom had rotted out, as had much of the leather saddles,
the lunging equipment, the bell boots, etc.
The whole thing smelled like sweet rot,
mushed away under our fingers
black and syrupy.

I think about this now
standing in the rotten house of my brain.
All this must go
and there is nowhere to rest or sit down
because I have not cleaned it yet.

All that horrible, sodden summer
I'd carry black waste out in armfuls,
the water slipping over the tops
of my rubber boots. I wanted to put it down –
put it all down, but everything was water
so I kept going.

# For Want of Prophecy in Delphi

My shoes were full
of stolen marble dust,
the grit of history,
bits of epic bone swirling in my lungs.
I thought, how dare I come here
with so few decades to my name?
Next year I will go to school,
and learn again that I know nothing.
How could I bring only that
to this enduring mountain,
with its gluttony of past?

But even that is washing away.
There are histories of art in the mud
like stew. The snake-god is gone.
The oracle is gone.
The rain fills her valley with silt.

In seven days from this day,
a farmer will tell me over bread and salt,
*only the first hundred years are hard.*
His voice will remind me of limestone,
chalky and chipped from years of smoking
and generations of fighting this daunting geography.

On this, child, build your future.

# The Exquisite Banality of Space

Interstellar space sounds like my finger on a wine glass –
whining, high and sharp, a choir we cannot identify.
I've listened to the recordings, here on our homeworld.

If I ever make it to that frontier
would that sound cut into my pink brain like a knife?
Would it open my skull like a wet rose?
Unlikely, my love. I bet I would be sick of it
pretty quickly.

Let us be bored of space, you and I.
Let us look out the window of our apartment
at the leaves we cannot count,
the stones the dinosaurs crushed to sand –
at the cosmic breath, posing as the gray mist of Tuesday morning –
and think, there must be more than this.

Make no mistake,
boredom is what moves us
from one triumph to the next.
Our minds hold awe like a wasp in a butterfly net.
No one knows how the thing we want flutters –
what petals it alights upon.

It's a dangerous thought for a Tuesday.
Will I tire of you, for instance?
Will there be a day when your hand on my back
doesn't spin my heart like red wine in a crystal glass?
Maybe. But then I'll find a new way
for you to touch me.

If I have a prayer,
it is that someday
something with blood like mine
hears that eerie melody in real time, sees the burning fires of stars
and is unimpressed before magnificent infinities –
moves on.

# The Rocket Falls to

the dirt
in the wound,
lemonade as we
watched the rockets tilt –
whoosh woosh kaboom!
And then
the silvery sauce,
redless, but full of endings.
At least we lived,
we said,
at least we are here on the
cold dead ground.
We would
never throw our hopes
so far – and the
yellow dog asleep
in the yard,
everything was
good good good
here on earth
when we never were
so far away,
but could be.

# Ponies and Rocketships

Ponies and rocketships are the blackest of magic
because they exist in your mind
beyond sin and debt,
a heroic nirvana of open ranges and deep space.

As little girls and little boys we believed we could have them
and we ran around the house with our fingers like rayguns
and our pink cowboy hats long before we understood
the complex historical and social ramifications
that made our dreams impossible.

People shoot mustangs now because they trample vegetables,
and light speed travel hasn't even been invented yet.

Ponies and rocketships are horrible things
because we have always watched movies
that tell us heroes ride ponies and rocketships
into suns, and we fell for it every time
and still hope we
will ride into suns and sunsets.

One day you realize it's impossible,
and also you will not be president.

My mother wished every Christmas
and ran out in the snow in her bare feet
while her mother called her an idiot
from the kitchen window.

She threw open the garage door and found
only her parents VW van and the little puddle of oil –
the old rusted tools that she would leave
for years after her father died.

She never found a pony or a rocketship
and neither will you.

What will actually happen is something like this:

you will get into the college of your choice, that you can't afford,
and the poet goddess of your department will call you practical
as if it's a contagious disease, and you will feel
like you have become a minor character.

You will find an uncomfortable peace in this and you will get very drunk
very often.
You will wake up next to people. You will walk

down dark alleys and get in at least one fist fight.
You will smash your head against the ground
and feel very strange for a day, but refuse
to go to a hospital. You'll be fine.

You will work much longer than you are being paid for.
You will be praised for your determination or not.
And you will play by the rules and still
not find a job to pay the money you owe and you will
wonder why you ever wanted to go to space
or chase outlaws in the first place.

You will wonder
what kind of debt *that* would have gotten you.

And then you might meet someone
and lie on the floor eating popcorn
because you can't afford a couch yet
and talk about a time when you will afford
so many couches.
You crush out the tiny fleas
and talk of a time when you won't
wage a tiny war across your carpet.

Yes, ponies and rocketships are the darkest of magic, because
the fantasy will creep back into your life
no matter how practical you are
or how little wine you drink
or how few times in your life

you allow yourself to use the word *yehaw*.

You will start thinking
of fighting space aliens again, maybe
driving home from work, at stop lights,
or pouring eggs into a saucepan, but you will
think of them again.

You will plan what you would do
if someone galloped into your living room,
stuck out their hand and said,
*There's no time!*

If you are lucky – if you have lived your life well –
you will think of the movies and the daydreams,
the hopes and disappointments with a surprised affection –

a nostalgia like that for your first shitty car
or ratty apartment –
as if you were the hero,
as if these were your war stories
and they are.

# Launch

The Kennedy Space Center
warned us
*you will feel it,*
*then you will hear it,*
*then you will see it,*
and it was like being
in the maternity ward,
strapped to the table
and his cry opening
into the world
like an iron rose
and I cried before
the barb of him
was even in my brain –
before I thought
*that is him*
before I saw him,
bloody red and roaring,
my heart was
already in his
sky.

# Weight

No astronaut has feared the unknown
like Eve looking at her belly,
larger and heavier each day.

What is this? What
is happening?

Please do not scream
at the sky. Some of it
will turn out okay.

You are only the second thing
in the whole universe
to make something new.

# Float

I'm starving for something with no name in my language –
something specific. Something that could fit
inside a blue bottle with a string around the neck.
The red trees are no comfort. They bleed
across the sidewalk. Fall is a time
of erasing boundaries. Everything
is suddenly all over the place.

It is terrifying to learn that you can own nothing.
A fire could claim the book of photos, our birth certificates.
I could toss out my name and claim a new one. You
could walk out the door and never return
and what leverage do I have on a heart?

The boy and I launch leaves onto the cold lake and
he wants his back. He cries as the little bit of maple tree
glides away from him. *I know*
I say. *I know.* I want
to go home and I am home.

# I Will Try to Describe

We discover physics like we write poetry –
marveling at a mystery
we already know –
to measure it,
to tell someone else
the dimensions
of our awe.

And yet I struggle
with words.
With focus.

I fall back on cliches.
I say I feel blessed
to be his mother,
even though
his hand is on my cheek
of his own volition.
Carried for nine months,
held while crying, while both crying,
and now a choice, a hand,
a new robin in the pine trees.

Our capacity for love
is always growing.
Is this why the universe expands?
It is filling with the awe we feel for it.

# Microbiome

I wonder what my microbes
have named me.
What are my national parks?
Do the bacteria
take little polaroids?
Buy souvenirs?
Please
love me.
I am trying
to be
a good
home.

# No Place for Us but the Place We Stand Upon

We own nothing but the things we claim –
shoeboxes of feathers and stones,
photos of what was wrong with us.

The shadows are long now, come inside.
Do you have a mother?
I'm your godmother now. The bees are singing
of what the clouds have made.

They drowned cats like us you know.
They shot mustangs who were just being there.
They buried the blood with the toe of their boot.

Look, here are dandelions.
You can eat them. You can blow them
to smithereens.

They know what we know and what we know
is nothing.
Only the sound that growing makes.
Only the few inches of earth under the roots
we made ourselves.

# Ars Fucking Poetica

My teachers told me to love this home
in which there is nowhere for me to sit,
no bed or chair or couch.

My teachers told me, *divorce the architect
from the rafters, the foundations,
the floorboards beneath your feet.*

The people who built this house would not have cared
if I liked it, if I felt warm. They did not see that as political.

Maybe they would have been alarmed at my ingress –
perhaps astonished – like someone seeing a dog
walk on their hind legs.

I hear the authors saying *Are you waiting for someone? Could you
wait outside? I don't remember unlocking that door.*

It is significant that the door is locked
and I had to come in through the window.
Let's discuss that I am standing,
that there is nowhere to rest –
that there is glass on the floor.

# Wonder Woman Visits the City

There are museums of antiquity
where people feel disconnected
to the blown glass,
the rough blade,
the golden massacre, a painting
of a deer in a church.

Their wars are
far away. No one
collects cotton
for bandages. No one
thinks of letters
like harbingers.

History is antlers before the alter.
Curated. Petrified.
Time itself, crushed against the wheel.

The city steals the banners
and mottos of
frightened and dying countries.
The people feel purified. The antlers –
the tile beside the painting explains –
symbolize hope.

I disagree.
The world is not new.
It is old and growing
older.

# Rey the Sister of My Strength

The lightsabers,
the wanting them,
and the not being allowed,
the hunger.

Power and light,
the newsprint ads, the comic books,
the Christmas gifts,
for smart boys, brave boys.

(The swords
on my brother's dresser,
his friends' dressers –
safe from me.)

Leia's immovable anger –
not enough. Put it
in her hands,
you cowards.

25 years –
the girl, the forest!
My husband, asking if I am okay.

I am not.
I am feasting and
sobbing. She has stolen it
for me.

The light is on her face.
The sword is in her hand.

# Loss Like Empty Seeds

I left the island of the glowing stones,
the moss-strangled shores, the birds
with trumpet flower heads;

I carried her on my back
for six miles after she fell,
crying that roots were growing
around her heart.

I didn't believe her
until I saw the creepers
break her skin, like caramel silk –
the little red flowers floating
in her blood.

I said, *Why is this happening?*
and she answered,
*There is no reason,* but I knew.

She had to see the island
of death in life, the leopards
with pollen falling from their eyes,
the serpents with stamen tongues,
the birds budding into trees –
to touch the trauma for a moment,
and it touched her back.

I reached our boat, but there were branches
parting her ribs, unknitting her veins,
lapping her up.

*We didn't make it. We didn't
make it,* she whispered, until her tongue
was a soft, red bud,
and her eyes bloomed green.

I went home, alone.

I carry that with me, a pollination
of my memory. The flowers
died on my porch. Only she
remembered to water them.
Only she remembered that life
is given
as easily as taken.

# A Spell

Close the circle.
It is closed.
The moment for choice
has passed.
You are too far.
The words are white
and red in your mind.
Why have you done this?
Why have you not
fed the hungry
or stopped
the bleeding
or built
something?

This poem is a spell
but so is
tomorrow
and now.

Go. Go.
I have given you
the power
you did not need.

# They Threw Tomato Soup on the Sunflowers

And my first feeling
was relief.
Yes
*Yes.*
Someone is doing something.

And, of course, it's a tragedy.
The floods are tragedies.
The fires.
I see the smoke even here in Ohio,
drinking thistle tea in my studio.
Some of that black cloud
is bodies – human.

Van Gogh ate foxglove to steady
his mental health. The same that grow
in my little garden under the smoke.
The same that will move north as the growing season
mutates.

My friend texted me after therapy on Monday,
*what medicine can I take for the end of the world?*
What flower should we eat?
Lotus, I suppose.

*Courage*, I told her. *For now, we are far from the sea.*

# Tell Me What the Stars Sing

There are sirens in the stars as in the sea.
They sing too, but we can't hear them.

Our ships record their frequencies
but not the sound
or words, if there are words.

What are the words?

We see the light ripple over
their slipstream, mirrored bodies.

We've lost so many people.
They threw themselves
into the void
for the same reason
they went to the stars –

they needed to know.
They needed
to know.

# Cassini

We have sent a fragile thing to space –
a thing made of mirrors and lightning,
a thing made of silver and gold
and time and strain and a force
we birth and cradle and fling
into the cosmos.

But now it is gone.

Does sadness have gravity?
Does it have a rotation?
Can you measure its physics?
And yet it is so real, so heavy.
It is a force we have built inside ourselves,
pulling our heart into its own, long orbit.

# Ballón de la Luna

Today the moon leapt
to Earth,
split along her seams
and filled the sky
with fire.
Ballerinas alone
had warning,
feeling the gravity change,
pulling their hands
up toward the red velvet.
For a moment,
they held the moon
in the horrified sky,
teetering on the edge
of beauty,
but it was too late.

Where are you now?
That is where you will be
at the end.
It doesn't matter
if you are proud
or if the moon
is sorry.

The moment
you were born
you were launched
through the galaxy
at 1.3 million miles per hour.
It is only a miracle
that this is the end
and not
any of the moments
before.

# Supergirl's Last Will and Testament

Clark, If you're reading this I am already
a mosaic of bone,
a green, flameless candle – dripping.
I knew the risks.

You told me once
when you were small and afraid of the dark,
you walked into the basement
and sat in the middle of the cement floor
until the fear was a thin broth
you could swallow.

I need you to do this now.

Imagine me as a copper, equine statue
with my hand outstretched, as if to say,
*Let's go that way for a while.*

Tell people I was too good for this planet.

I was not. They
are not.
What is grief
but a love that is
too vast for us?

Imagine me lost with our homeworld. Imagine me
splattered. Imagine me taking flight, rolling sideways
under a plane's sleek, silver back
and disappearing up into its engines.

Imagine me, facing the hunger
between the stars,
dancing between
its teeth.

Imagine my end as the dark. Drink it
as slowly as you must
so you won't be afraid.

# Divine

Angels are
horrifying, jointed
in multiples, red
and burning.

They cannot feel
anything but what
they feel.

Their wings,
pinioned in gold,
sharp to the touch –
their crowns, too heavy,
bow their heads.

They do not know
the name of their God
or your name
or the names of any
thing.

They know the words
to speak only as they
are speaking.

There is a single moment,
always,
after the last word
leaves their lips
that they almost
understand its meaning.

They yearn. They
*yearn.*
They want it back
so they can cherish it
as you cannot.

They would destroy you,
pull the word, wet
and dripping
from your lungs.

But the darkness
passes.
Again, their wings
cut the air –
they sing.

# The Plagues

The world is going to hell, I swear to God.
The early hail is wandering into locusts
and my rash is acting up again,
but that's not the worst of it.

At least the frogs were starting to die off.
Last night I did nothing
but sweep their green bodies through the door,
somersaulting like acrobats.

There is no point in cleaning anymore.
The stalls are empty. The horses are dead.

I liked the horses, the thin chariot horses built like herons,
the stocky, plough horses made of rock.
They were all simple and gentle.
Anything that size that doesn't break you on sight
is being gentle.

Now I sweep their empty stalls.
But what else can I do? Should I go down
to the Papyrus Bar? Should I say,
*Hey guys. It has been a crazy week
and I could really use a drink! Haha.*

Maybe we could avoid talking about
how we've washed little bits
of other people off our hands –
their decaying skin like wet moths.

Maybe we can talk about the fact
that the river is the wrong color.

Worst of all was when the livestock went.
That's the thing I don't understand, really.
I mean they didn't do anything, with their big eyes
and their clumsy strength.

I liked them. They were warm
and liked seeing you. Liked seeing anything.
Liked grass and trees and just standing there.
I'm not sure why they had to die.

A half an hour ago someone ran through the street, yelling
*the city is burning and the king's son is dead!*
But who cares? I guess I'm having
an existential crisis is all.

I don't think I could believe in a god
who could do this.

# Werewolf's Aubade

Before I met him I was a wolf.
With the sun he rolled me over,
his cool hands on my hot gut.

He said, *Good morning.*
*I still love you.*

I remember the moonlight like naked silver
through my skin, my muscles,
glinting off bone, but that's all.

I told him *I'm afraid*
*I'll wake up one day and be my mother.*

He rolled his eyes.
*You can't just change like that.*

I tried to leave but he held me. I said,
*I'll bite you. I'll tear your collarbones out.*

He said, *No you won't.*

*I'll change. I'll make you hate me.*

*No. You won't.*

*I'm a wolf.* I said. *I'm a wolf. I'm a wolf!*

*No.* He said. *I will tell you what you are.*

# Center

Space travel is accomplished by a few human bodies,
but powered always by a vast history,
an enormous present,
an incalculable future of people looking
up, up, UP.

Does the universe love us?
It made us.
It keeps us.
It surrounds us.
It waits for us to reach for it.
It reaches back.

What other love is there?

We are not at the center of the universe,
and yet we can only observe it outwards - from ourselves.
If you close your eyes
you can feel it swing around you,
the fulcrum of the cosmos.

# The Encyclopedia of Completely Normal Planets

There is a planet with one eye.
There is a planet with a thousand eyes.
There are planets full of reaching hands and curious minds.
There is a planet whose creatures consider only their own dirt.

There is a planet that in the billions of years of creation
managed to only produce a single creature –
roughly a crab, made of glass,
shy and glittering and impeccable.

There is a planet with a night sky that knows your name.
There is a planet on which names are a contagion.
There is a planet with a single cell
reborn again and again.
There is a planet with a red sun.
There is a planet with a transparent moon,
filled with cracks as long as the Earth.

There are planets with 82 moons.
There are planets where it rains diamonds.
There are planets with supersonic winds.
There are planets where water flows
all day and night
and millions of species live and grow.

For now, we can only imagine our siblings - born in the searing explosion,
waiting patiently with us, to inherit eternity.

# The Pig, Wilbur, to His Grandsons

She sang
when she thought
we were asleep.
The sound was like
when the screen door
tore off the house in the storm,
like the crying of the killdeer
when the farmer plows over
their nests.

I was so afraid,
and how did she understand
the words – the human words,
with their hands that smell
like blood?

We don't know why
she helped us,
why she gave her short time
to me, small and pink and afraid.

We have to hope
it was for good reasons.

# Potato Song

You sang before you could talk,
wandering around the kitchen with a potato,
(where did you find a potato?)
holding a single note, high and flat and long.
*I want to know what that word is*, your grandfather says,
but I don't think it's a word yet –
just the feeling of song in your throat
like holding something you probably shouldn't have
and you can't remember where you found.

They say memory begins with language,
but you already remember me –
my voice, my calm in the dark, my rules about the trashcan.
Language is how we order things –
the boxes we put our world in,
a feeble attempt to hold a potato up to the world and say
*look* and
*heavy*
and *lovely*
and
*mine.*

# Eulogy for Spirit and Opportunity

The rovers are dying on Mars.
Their springs and bolts and cogs drop
into the red sand.
Their cameras clog with dirt. Their wheels freeze.
They limp up hills and spread their solar panels
like hospital blankets.
The technicians do not tell them
about the budget cuts, or the questions of purpose.
They say, everything here is fine.
Write if you find water.

That is progress, and progress
isn't supposed to be sad.

I will always live in a world where a man
has walked on the moon.

I love you, Mars rovers,
for traveling so far, as far as you could.
Till your joints filled with the dust of strange places,
and your signals dragged themselves home
to tell us the wonderful news –
there is still no end of the world.

# They Didn't Hate You Because You Read Comics

or hung spaceships
from your ceiling
or collected small dolls
with delicate swords
or played games from books
or read books about games.

They stole your lunch because
you were weird
like me, a bubble
off center, unable to be still,
pulling at your hair, chewing
your nails,
tortured by the things
that happened at home,
or just the uneven beating
of your own heart –

or you were poor.
There were holes in your socks.
You couldn't get the sports
lunchbox or the butterfly clips.

There is nothing
you could have done
correctly enough.

Or maybe it was because
you were mean and sharp –
a curled hedgehog
full of fear and spines.

But it wasn't the comics.
If you hadn't had comics
they would have found
something else you loved
to hurt you.

I'm not trying
to steal anything
from you.
I know they were
a lightness – a white cloud.

I tell you this
to bring you peace –
to tell you that I see you,
a very small ship
guiding yourself with the stars
you could see.
You should
be proud.

# Big Bang

I have created life
and thus, I am
a very small universe,
one that is
inexplicably
self-determinable.
So, I shall name
my own constellations.
The pain in my knee
I shall name *Pine*
and *Ice*
for my childhood.
The worry
tucked under my eyes
*Fragments from*
*the Book of the Dead,*
and this thin, white moon
on my abdomen
I will name *Us*.
*Sigh in the Dark,*
my fingers
on your back
as it rises and falls –
this is the orbit of my life –
each movement
the beginning.

# Deerborn

When I was five my parents
had my horns removed. They told
their friends that I had fallen
learning to walk. I wore the scabs
like a crown of rubies.

The other children knew. We touched
our foreheads with tiny fingers in salute.

They painted the ragged fences white.
The old farmhouse caught fire.
Jason said he saw the hawks circle
the smoke for three days and nights.

The trees tiptoed in at night,
slid their roots into the charcoal, like fingers
into secret, black hair. Their bark was white.
We grew with them, in uneasy air.
We came out wild.

The schools kept us in tights and charcoal shoes.
The schools told us not to run, to line up.

At night we stole our fathers' hunting rifles,
opened bedroom windows,
loud as nervous cats, slinking through the forests,
ashes up to our ankles.

We built fires together and ran through the dust,
slamming our heads together, striking off sparks.
I waited my turn, slid my fingers into the dark –
found something reaching back.

# Not Helen but the Thing that Held Her

*Throne Room*
Helen sat in the center of me.
She hated the flowers they brought her.
She knew that soon her subjects
would start stabbing each other with kitchen knives
just for something to do. She was not stupid.
So when the offer came from a beautiful prince
she flew off like a thin, white bird.
And I was proud of her,
though the walls were afraid.

*Tower*
Feet carry water up my stairs.
Out the window, a field of amaranth
innocent of horse hooves.
Feet have carried water to the top of my stairs
all my life, and poured it down
to clean my insides.
There is something alive
and chained in my foundations
that no one remembers
to feed.

*Walls*
The flowers keep me up,
little night terrors of the earth –
small and growing
growing, growing, growing, growing
into my sides- Oh god!
I want to fly too. I am stuck
in this field, wearing the sky for a hat,
glancing out under the brim
at the universe. Naked but made of stone.
Prove to me I will be a ruin.
Prove to me the king will return.
Someone pours water down my throat.
Clean the walls! Wash the stairways!
The queen ran away, but soon! but soon!

everything will be set rightly on fire.

    *Moat.*
The men and women sit on my bridge and pray
for ships and wind and the blood
that brings the ships and the wind.
I pray for no white horses. No bells.
If the king comes I will fill my moat with fire.
I will lock all my doors and never let him leave.
But even now, I hear the stems of the purple flowers
breaking under the iron horseshoes.
I am only the thing he will see first.

# Siren Song

We do not lure.
We do not lure.

We are here
and we are singing,
just as we have always been here,
singing, singing to the gulls,
the surf, the green, green eyes
of the ones we love,
beside us, beside us,
their skin on our skin,
their smell of salt and gentleness.

      The boats came. The boats came.
Came for us, wanted us,
were broken. They showered us
in splinters and blood,
but we were only
            singing, singing.

Do not blame our skin, our song.
        You were ruined the moment you felt
    we were for you.

# The Ghost of an Astronaut Talking to the Ghost of a Cowgirl

*Goddamn I could use a drink.* The Captain says.
*How long do you figure? Till the second coming?*

*Hell, that already happened* says the Cowgirl.
*I met a son of God once at the Red Pass, his pony was thin
and mad, his ears worn back.
We let him sleep beside us, but I stayed awake
all night and watched him. The world was lousy
with knives and bullets. All I needed
was one between my ribs. In the morning,
I saw his body rise against the sky,
like he was going to lift it with the top of his head
and then he shot me, and then all of us. Left with our horses
without even kicking over the fire.
And the prairie burned, all those trails
I once knew. Now that pass
is named after his fucking horse.
That was the second coming.*

*No* the Astronaut says. *Can't be.
I died after you. My ship nicked an asteroid.*

*After the hull collapsed, after my nerves failed, I wanted
to know, even then, the calculations of the gyre of my opening body –
wide to an incomprehensible universe like a woman
undressing for a man she loves and knows
cannot love her, a shapeless, horrid excitement –
a shuddering. Who can be called great but us?*

# As Salmon Swim Upstream

When astronauts close their eyes in space,
the radiation from the sun plays
across their optic nerves
like golden ghosts.

Our minds interpret the energy
of the universe as art,
even when we're trying not to see.

# Acknowledgements

"Deerborn" was originally published in *Shock Totem*, March 2014.

"Werewolf's Aubade" was originally published in *Apex*, September 2014.

"Loss Like Empty Seeds" was originally published in *Asimov's*, March 2015.

"The Exquisite Banality of Space" was originally published in *Uncanny*, September 2015.

"Sleeping Beauty Attains Bliss" was originally published in *Asimov's*, January 2015.

"Heavenly Body" was originally published in *Asimov's*, June 2018.

"Tell Me What The Stars Sing" was originally published in *Star\*Line*, February 2018.

"Ballon de la Luna" was originally published in *Andromeda Spaceways*, February 2019.

"The Pig, Wilbur to his Grandsons" was originally published in *Asimov's*, November 2020.

"Supergirl's Last Will and Testament" was originally published in *Strange Horizons*, September 2020.

"The Valley of Midas" was originally published in *Strange Horizons*, February 2020.

"Goodbye Homeworld" was originally published in *Analog*, July 2020.

"Launch" was originally published in B*oston Literary Magazine*, July 2020.

"The Most Original Sin" was originally published in *8 Poems*, February 2020.

"Divine" was originally published in *Star*Line*, February 2021.

"Magical Girl Transformation" was originally published in *Star*Line*, February 2021.

"Supergirl Doesn't Look at the stars" was originally published in *Asimov's*, March 2022.

# About the Author

Leslie J. Anderson lives in a small, white house beside a cemetery with her husband, son, three good dogs, and a Roomba. Her writing has appeared in Asimov's, Uncanny Magazine, Strange Horizons, Daily Science Fiction, and Apex to name a few. She has a Creative Writing M.A. from Ohio University and is currently working as a marketing and communications manager for a healthcare data analytics firm. Her favorite flower is foxglove.

Author Website: www.lesliejanderson.com

Twitter: @inkhat

Facebook: /lesliejandersonwriter

Instagram: @lesliejandersonwriter

Printed in Great Britain
by Amazon